THE
GREAT
ZOO HUNT!

PIPPA UNWIN

DOUBLEDAY
NEW YORK LONDON TORONTO SYDNEY AUCKLAND

Published by Doubleday, a division of Bantam Doubleday Dell Publishing Group, Inc., 666 Fifth Avenue, New York, New York 10103   Doubleday and the portrayal of an anchor with a dolphin are trademarks of Doubleday, a division of Bantam Doubleday Dell Publishing Group, Inc.   Library of Congress Cataloging-in-Publication Data   Unwin, Pippa.   The great zoo hunt!/Pippa Unwin.—1st ed.   p. cm.   Summary: The reader is asked to help the zookeeper locate ten escaped animals in the detailed illustrations.   [1. Zoo animals—Fiction. 2. Picture puzzles.] I. Title.   PZ7.U444Gr 1990   [Fic]—dc20   89-33817   CIP   AC   ISBN 0-385-41106-5   ISBN 0-385-41107-3 (lib. bdg.)   Copyright © 1989 by Pippa Unwin   All Rights Reserved   First Edition in the United States of America, 1990   0690

Here is a small town by the sea. In the town there is a zoo.
Can you see it?

This is a story about that zoo and the new zookeeper who
nearly got into trouble.

If you look at the pictures carefully you can help him set
things right.

This is the zoo.

Yesterday the new zookeeper started work.

4

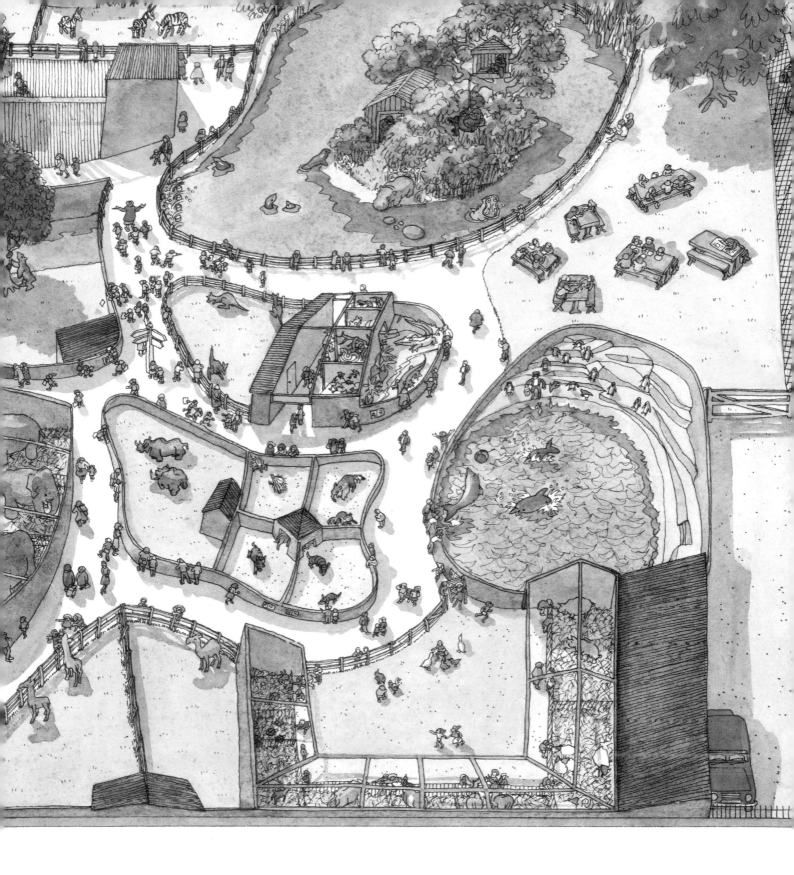

Can you see him feeding the dolphins and the penguins?

At the end of the day, the new zookeeper had to feed the
animals and make sure they were all safe inside their
cages.

He gave them their food and he thought he had locked all the doors and gates, but the next day, when he got to work...

. . . he found ten of the animals were missing!

"Oh dear!" he said. "They've escaped! Where are the camel and the elephant? Where have the giraffe, the hippo, and

8

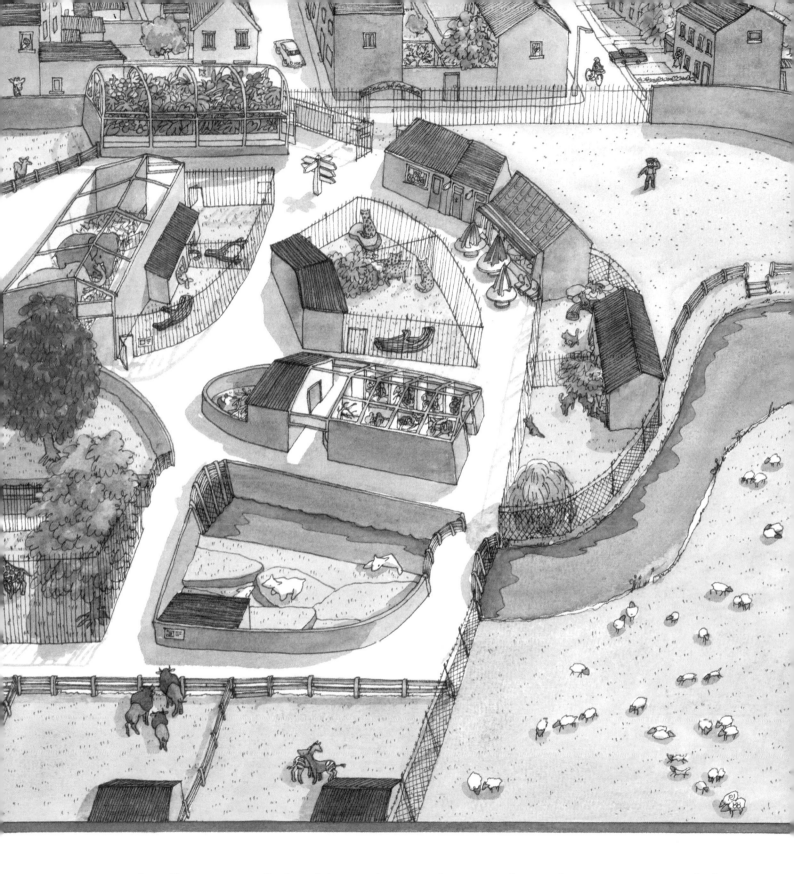

the lion gone? And I can't see the monkey, the parrot, and the snake — or the tiger and zebra."

Can *you* help the zookeeper find the animals?

9

Perhaps one of the animals is hiding in the market place.

Can you see one of the animals in this street?

Who is sleeping in the town square?

Perhaps one of the animals is here.

Can you help the zookeeper find it?

17

18

Is an animal hiding among the houses?

Lots of people are enjoying themselves in the park.

Is one of the animals there too?

What is hiding at the swimming pool?

Is there an animal in the gardens?

Will the zookeeper find an animal at the beach?

Just one more animal to find!

The keeper is very pleased.

He has all the animals now.

parrot

monkey

elephant

camel

tiger

Did you help him to find each of them?

There is just enough time to put them all back in the zoo before it opens.

giraffe

hippo

zebra

lion

snake

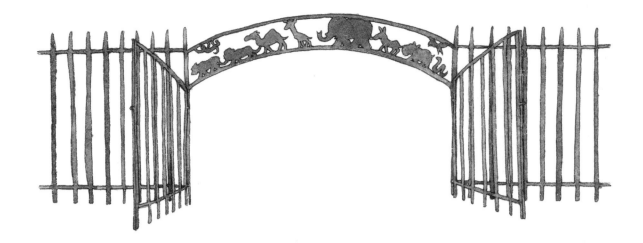

Now all the animals are safely back.

"Thank you very much for helping me," says the keeper.
"I'd never have found them on my own."

PRINTED IN BELGIUM BY
INTERNATIONAL BOOK PRODUCTION

A New Hunt

Now that all the animals have been safely returned to the zoo, turn back to the beginning of the book, to the picture of the whole town. The dotted line shows the route the zookeeper took.

If you look again through the other pictures, you will find some of the things the zookeeper saw while he was searching for the animals — and some that he didn't!

For instance, on page 4, can you see the children riding on the elephant?

Turn to page 10 and see if you can find the dog that is stealing the sausages. And where is the boy who is giving flowers to a girl?

In the school playground, the children are playing lots of different games. How many can you recognize?

In one picture you can see sheep escaping. Can you find them being rounded up in another picture?

What does the postman ride on when he is delivering letters?

The window cleaner is also in most of the pictures. Can you find him helping to rescue a cat?

If you follow the zookeeper on his search, there are more things to look for in the pictures —I hope you have fun finding them!

Pippa Unwin